Fields of Lavender in Provence

This Belongs to

Joal Donovan

Gift of Marie & Vianney Bollier

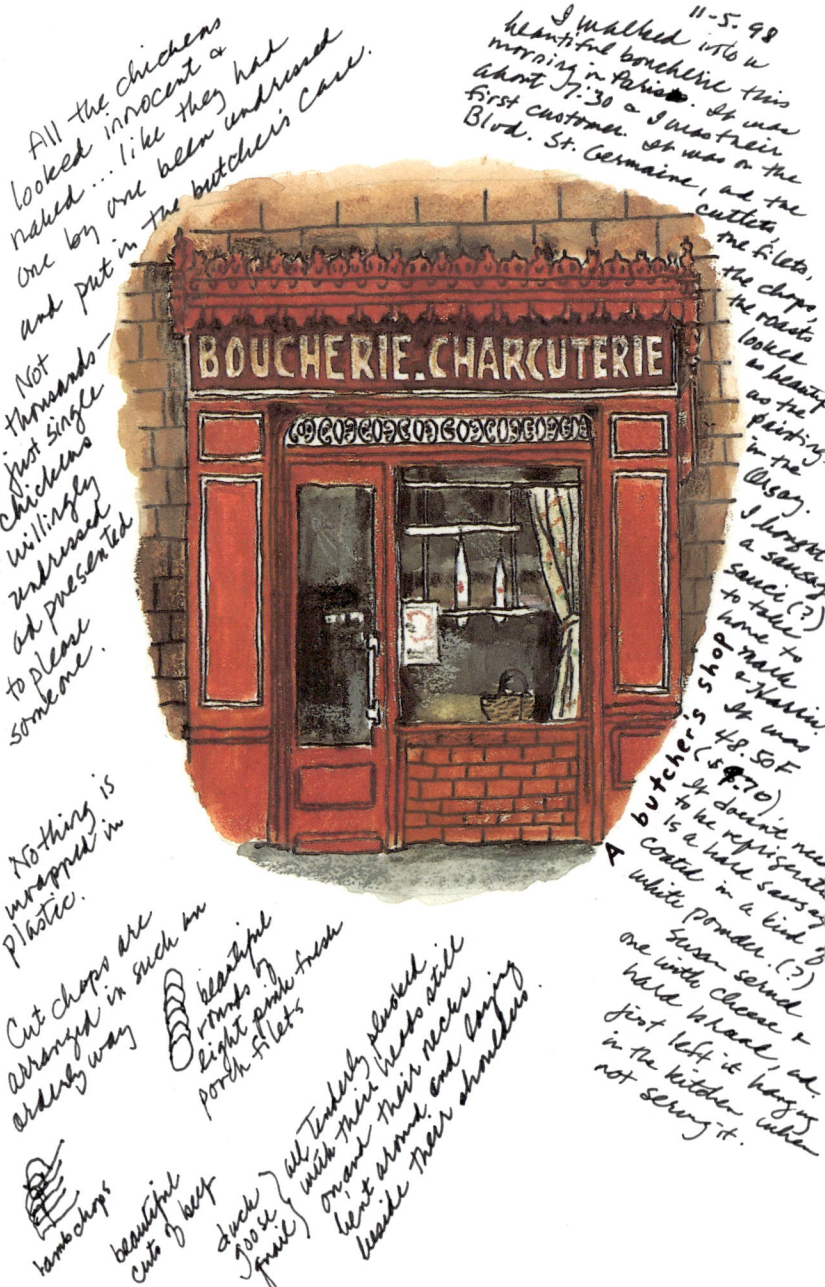

11-5-98

I walked into a beautiful boucherie this morning in Paris. It was about 7:30 a I was their first customer. It was on the Blvd. St. Germaine, and the cutlets, the filets, the chops, the roasts looked as beauty as the paintings in the Orsay. I bought a saussi (?) to take home to Noelle a Kasin. It was 48.50F (≈$8.70). It doesn't need to be refrigerated. It is a hard sausag coated in a kind of white powder. (?) Susan Sehnd one with cheese & hard bread, ad first left it hanging in the kitchen when not serving it.

All the chickens looked innocent & naked ... like they had one by one been undressed and put in the butcher's case.

Not thousands — just single chickens willingly undressed at presented to please someone.

Nothing is wrapped in plastic.

Cut chops are arranged in such an orderly way.

beautiful rounds of light pink fresh pork filets

lamb chops

beautiful cuts of beef

ducks? all tenderly plucked 300 E with their heads still on and their necks bent around and laying beside their shoulders.

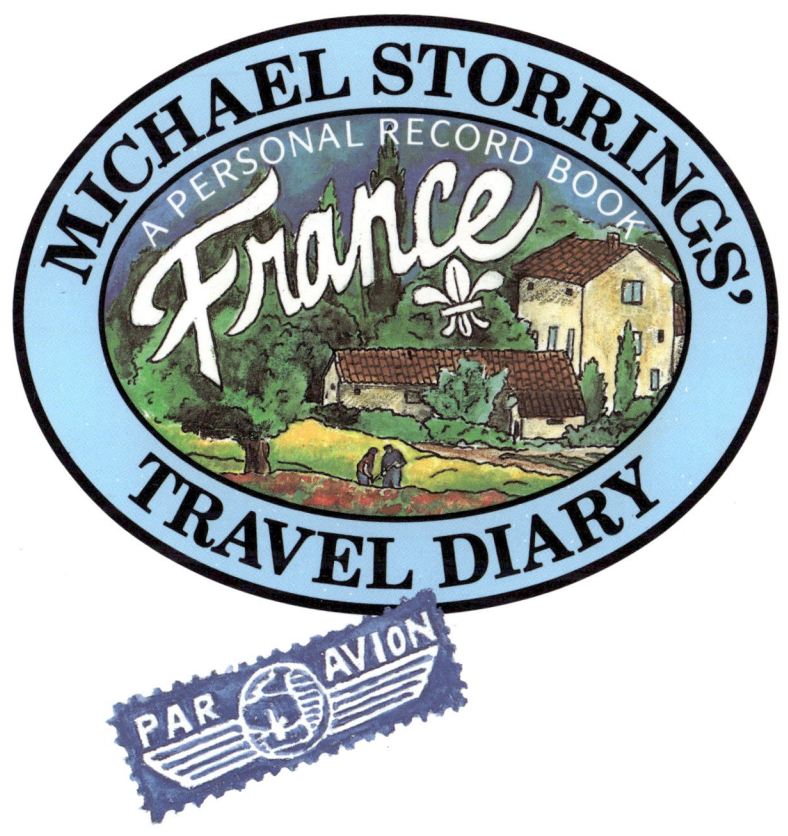

WARNER TREASURES™
PUBLISHED BY WARNER BOOKS
A TIME WARNER COMPANY

Copyright © 1995 by Michael Storrings
All rights reserved

Warner Treasures is a trademark
of Warner Books, Inc.

Warner Books, Inc.
1271 Avenue of the Americas
New York, N.Y. 10020

W A Time Warner Company

Printed in China

First Printing: March 1995
10 9 8 7 6 5 4 3 2 1
ISBN: 0-446-91001-5

TABLE OF CONTENTS

TRAVEL ITINERARY................6
BUDGET........................8
THINGS MY FRIENDS WANT ME TO DO AND SEE...10
THINGS TO BRING BACK FOR MY FRIENDS AND FAMILY...11
HOTELS AND INNS................12
RESTAURANTS...................20
NEW FRIENDS...................28
LES CAFÉS.....................30
NIGHTLIFE.....................32
THEATER.......................34
SHOPPING NOTES................36
SIGHTSEEING...................42

Travel

Sat 10/24/98 Ellington Field to Intercontinental
Sun 10/25 (Harris' B'Day) Arrive Paris 11:00 am. (+/-)
 Marie Juanchick Bollier & Lili meet us at the airport.
 We have coffee + croissants together & visit.
1:30 - 6:00 Train to Sainte

10/25 - 10/27 Sainte   Robert, Susan & Harris Lynch
                         19, rue Charles Danjibeau

10/28 drive through

Itinerary 7

Où est la gare?

Budget 8

Everything in France is expensive. Who can have a budget?

Continental breakfast in the hotel in Paris was $10. a piece. Cokes are $3. Newsweek magazine was $5.

The breads I bought to take home were 54F ($11) for 8 croissants + 1 pain de campagne.

The museum pass (Carte de Musée) was 180F ... no, I think 160F ($32). <u>A bargain.</u> It got us into every museum

- Louvre
- D'Orsay
- Museum of Modern Art
- Sainte Chappelle
- Conciergerie
- L'Orangerie
- Arc de Triomphe
- Caimondo

IN FRANCE the currency is the Franc. There are 100 centimes in one FRANC.

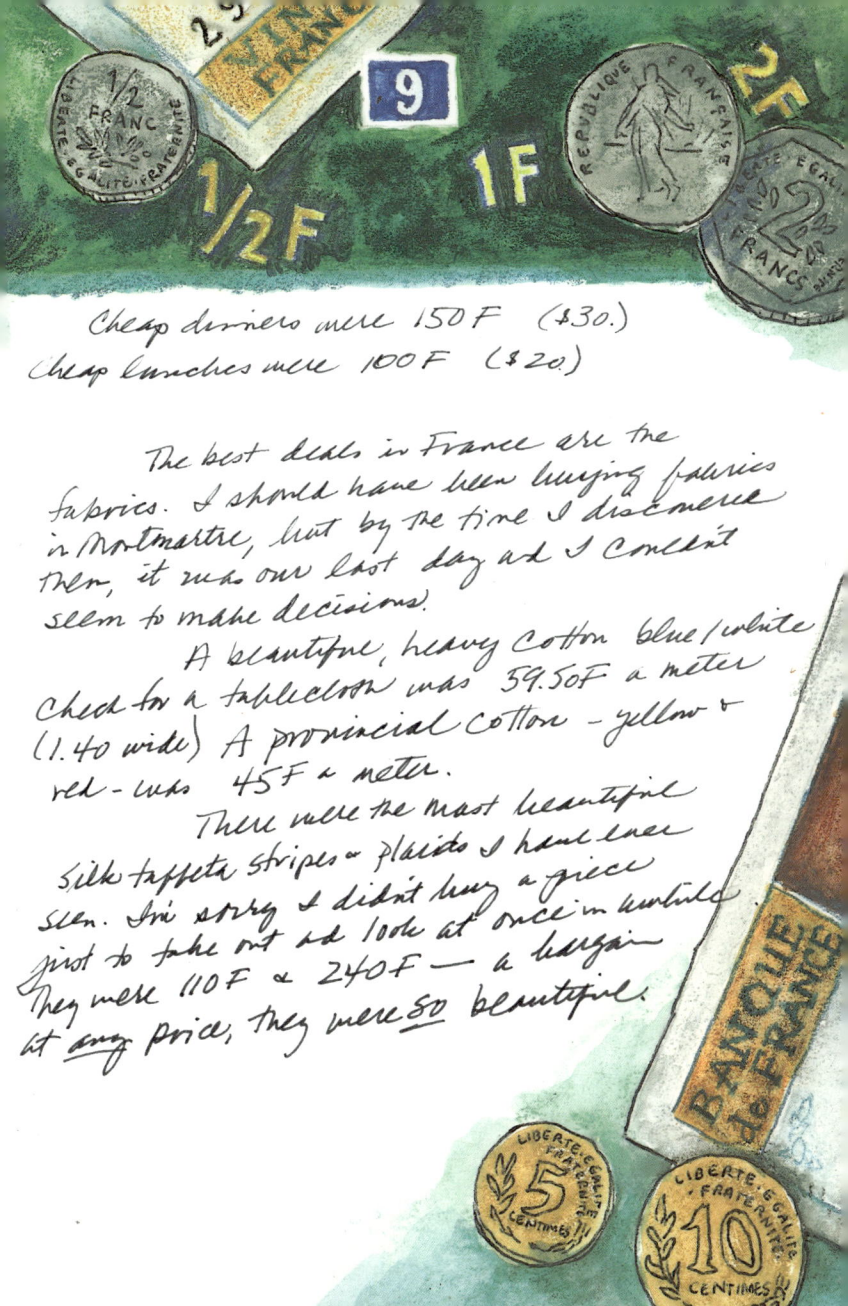

Cheap dinners were 150F ($30.)
Cheap lunches were 100F ($20.)

The best deals in France are the fabrics. I should have been buying fabrics in Montmartre, but by the time I discovered them, it was our last day and I couldn't seem to make decisions.

A beautiful, heavy cotton blue/white check for a tablecloth was 59.50F a meter (1.40 wide) A provincial cotton — yellow & red — was 45F a meter.

There were the most beautiful silk taffeta stripes & plaids I have ever seen. I'm sorry I didn't buy a piece just to take out and look at once in awhile. They were 110F & 240F — a bargain at any price, they were SO beautiful.

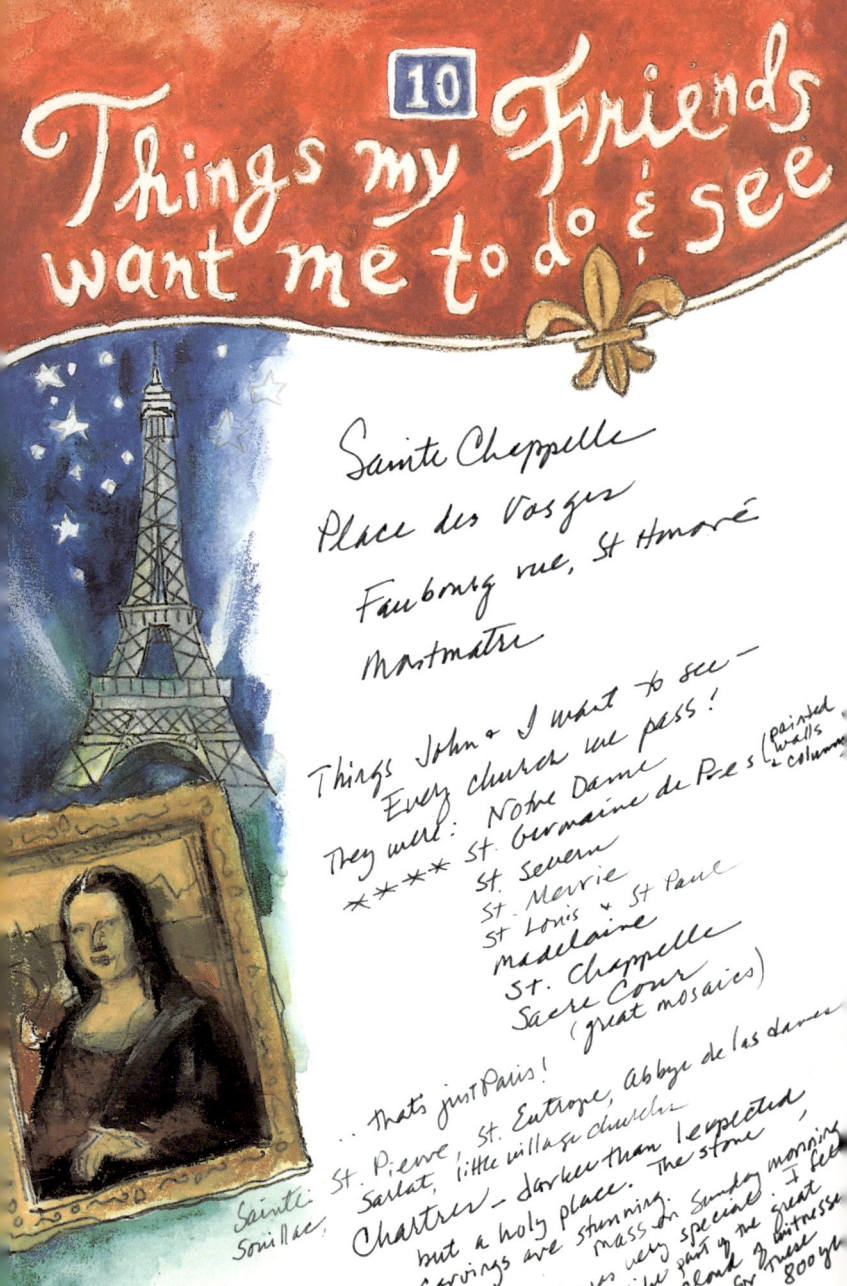

10 Things my Friends want me to do & see

Sainte Chappelle
Place des Vosges
Faubourg rue, St Honoré
Montmatre

Things John & I want to see —
Every church we pass!
They were: Notre Dame
*** St. Germaine de Pres (painted walls & columns)
St. Severin
St. Mervie
St Louis & St Paul
Madelaine
St. Chappelle
Sacre Cour
(great mosaics)

... that's just Paris!
Sainte Souillac, St. Pierre, St. Eutrope, Abbye de las dames
Sarlat, little village churches
Chartres — darker than I expected, but a holy place. The stone carvings are stunning. Mass on Sunday morning was very special. I felt like part of the great cloud of witnesses for these 800 yr

I made a kind of vow to myself not to bring back things because France is too expensive.

But. I bought some buttons for mother's sweater. A few narrow ribbons. (for me?)

Quimper tin wear for Sally & Susan (the best buy in the country)

Cards of one sort or another for Christmas (from Chartres) - 3 paper bookmarks (wish I had bought 10.!)

I bought one antique - a porcelain enamel trivet in Chartres. A deal 40F ($8)

I'm bringing Mark & Harris hotel shower gel & soap, a tin of mints, and croissants, bread & sausage for supper.

Le Parfum

Herbes de Provence

Get Joan's shirt size!

Things to Bring back for my Friends & Family

12 HOTELS & INNS

The favorite experience: Gran Coderc
        Mr. et Mdm. Gaillard (Monique et Bern
   a Gîte rural. (Their farm)

The Stone house was 300 yrs old. The three legged dog greeted us on arrival. We were shown to the room & my heart fell. It reminded me of the tacky Irish B&B's. An extra bed had a blue bedspread on it made out of what looked like hair. But it <u>was</u> clean.

Monique showed us the room — then showed us the dining room. There were four longish tables. Places were set for over 20 people. I was amazed. She had served that many for lunch, and now she was going to serve that many for dinner.

We had had a big lunch in a little village

Avez-vous une chambre libre?

JTEL DES
ARRONIERS
TARIF
★ ★ ★

Douche 2 lits
ou 2 personnes... 650F
Petit déjeuner 42F
t supplémentaire... 170F
     IX NETS

HOTEL DES ANGES

13

On the road — great pork roast, peas & carrots, salad with goat cheese on toast and some kind of incredibly rich raspberry/cream extravaganza.

We told Monique we couldn't eat a big meal. TOO BAD. It turned out she was cooking foix gras in the coals of her enormous fireplace — which had a fire going when we arrived about 5:00. She was also serving Magret du Canard. (Also roasted on the fire)

John & I & the three legged dog went on a long walk — medieval houses in the little lanes — we wandered down one lane & came across two men & their still. They were making Eau de vie, and they looked like two characters right out of "Jean de Florette".

Dinner was served at 8:00. What a production! Monique — red short hair & a kind of crisp face — had put on make-up & high heels. She was in charge. A young girl (20's or so) helped her. Bernard was the entertainment.

14

We started out with a potage — kind of a dark broth with large beans and toasted French bread floating in it.

Next — we had a quiche & country potatoes. Our other tablemates had the same. Everyone else was French. Our tablemates were from Toulon on the coast. About our age — they had their young granddaughter Manon with them. They made a pallet on the floor by their end of the table, and Manon slept through the 3-hr meal.

The others — couples, families, a mother & daughter, two single men — were served other things. One table had sauerkraut, sausage & pork. All the others had Foie Gras on toast — followed by a duck breast wrapped around duck liver & mushrooms & smothered, served in a sauce. Their next course was the magret du canard with country potatoes & pain de campagne — heavy & coarse & to die for. Dessert — a kind of omelet — which was covered in brandy & lit.

Je voudrais une chambre

15

Monsieur Gaillard told me story after another. A colossal kind of man in both size and temperament — a colossal raconteur also. Everyone was howling with laughter — even John & I, although we didn't understand a thing. Mon. Gaillard's style was infectious — his joie, contagious. The fire was warm, the language was intoxicating, the wine was flowing, the people were happy — truly happy. It was like being at some medieval banquet.

The man at our table wanted to know how we had ever found out about this place. (Bureau de Tourisme in Terrasson.) Pure luck. Pure enchantment. A magic night.

Next morning at breakfast I noticed a framed magazine article about the Gaillards. One of the guests — a man from St. Tropez came into breakfast. He was going with Mr. Gaillard on his tractor later in the morning.

It was obvious that the sophisticated & wealthy come to Gros Codere to get a taste of the earthy. Simple pleasures.

La clef

And the best bargain of the trip.

Room 120 F
Breakfast 20 F ea
Dinner 45 F ea
"You didn't eat much, Madame" Gaillard said.

Chambre

Petit déjeuner.... 33
Téléphone.....
1 chambre.... 240
Montant à payer
Hôt
21 Rue de

PLACE BUSINESS CARDS HERE

PLACE BUSINESS CARDS HERE

PLACE POSTCARD HERE

PLACE POSTCARD HERE

21

The man who maybe owned the place — thick grey very straight hair — longish — A square kind face. Thick <u>black</u> eyebrows.

 Was she his wife? The lonely lady in black — very black hair, a well made-up face. Very proper, but with a fine smile. Every sentence starting or ending in "Madame". She took the order and seemed so pleased when I ordered the Magret du Canard.

 The waitress was reed thin. No uniforms here. She wore her short beige wool skirt & long sweater over it. Her hair was short — the same color & she wore thin rimmed glasses. She was so efficient; she looked no nonsense; but she had a nice sense of humor & smiled often & easily.

 We sat in the window. It was a teeny place — others were dining, too. It was intimate & cozy and everyone seemed to be taken care of in almost a familial way by the kind, square-faced man, the lonely woman and the cheerful young waitress. She didn't seem to be a waitress. She seemed a good friend who happened to be serving us.

La fourchette

La cuillère

Une bouteille du vin

Le couteau

23

Le poisson

L'entrecôte avec les pommes frites

The Boulangeries — The Patisseries.
In every town, city, a village. On every block — there is a least one — often two — everywhere — an art form. bread is

In fact — they are called Boulangerie Artesanal.

They are too beautiful — these rows of croissants, brioches, pains de pays, tartes, eclairs, things I don't even know.

Sometimes all I could do was just "tear up" I couldn't hold all the beauty that was Les France. desserts

PLACE BUSINESS CARDS HERE

PLACE BUSINESS CARDS HERE

30

Les Cafés

Monsieur, je voudrais...

32 Nightlife

36 Shopping Notes

RT 1 225.00
TOTAL 225.00
ESPÈCES 225.00
MERCI DE VOTRE VISITE
LE 05/10/01 A 17H30

Blanc

Bleu

Vert

Rouge

Jaune

Noir

Dress Sizes

U.S.	6	8	10
France	36	38	40

38

Les Santons de Provence

Marché aux fleurs

Celui-ci = this one

39

La Poterie de Provence

Celui-là = that one

PLACE BUSINESS CARDS HERE

PLACE BUSINESS CARDS HERE

A speed limit sign in km/h

MONET'S GARDENS IN GIVERNY

51

Bistrot de Breteuil - the last supper
  $182F Prix fixe
 aperitif - champagne = kir
 John - Foie Gras   / Joal Seafood & cheese
                    hot (chaud) shrimp, oysters,
                    salmon white fish
                    in a sauce = cheese. Rich!

Lamb chops = frites
 & haricots vertes

A bottle of Bordeaux rouge

Creme Brûlée
Café

All inclusive. (I found it in a book)

a zillion cars were being towed away as we left the restaurant

Tow-away zone

AXE ROUGE

ARRÊT GENANT

John had wandered during dinner to take a photo, yelling till the lights went out

Small
Took the métro to
 Duroc
Lots of French men &
families, but several
Americans. The people at the next
table looked French - young, good-looking
& sounded American.
Aaron & Amy Grenader
 Grenadier? Attractive & friendly.

France is a country of shutters.

related to the Forbes Houston!

52

METRO TICKETS

We had a Paris pass for transportation for 3 days. We bought it at the train station at the CDG airport when we arrived. I don't remember how much it cost — but it was worth every Franc.

We must have ridden 1000 subways. Our main metro stops for boarding were D'Orsay & Assemblé Nationale. We were less than a block from each of them. Hotel Orsay is a _fine_ location.

Other stops I especially remember names of: "St. Michel - Notre Dame"
"Concorde"
"Charles De Gaulle Etoile"
"Père Lachaise"
"Franklin D. Roosevelt"
"Monceau" (that beautiful park with those beautiful babies)
"Pigalle"

"Abesses"   "Bastille"   "Hôtel de Villes"
"Sevres-Babylone"   "Duroc"

    I loved seeing the Nouveau ironwork at the entrance to the Metro at Monceau. It was just like the photo in my French book when I was a freshman in college.

    The metros are full of strolling musicians: accordian players, especially, all trying to make a centime or two.

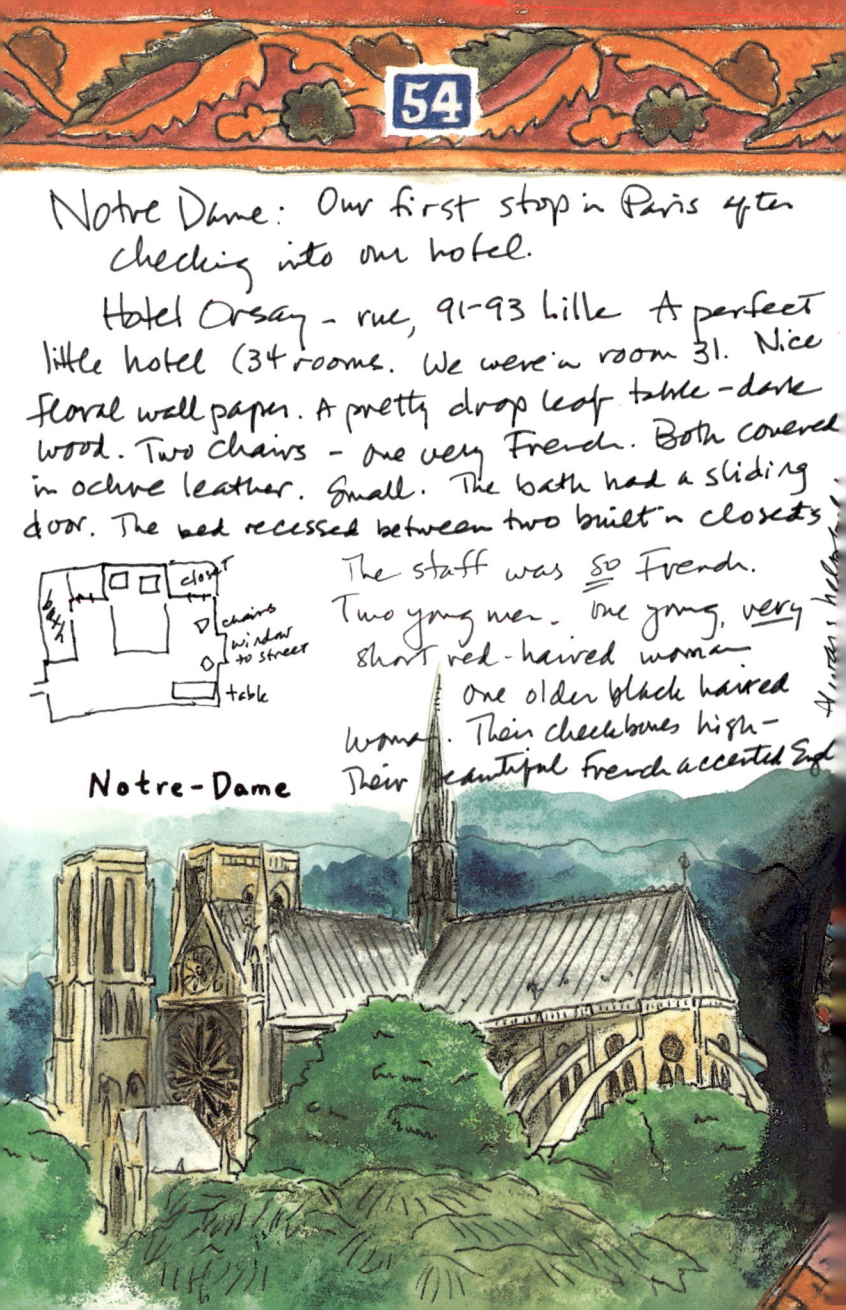

Notre Dame: Our first stop in Paris after checking into our hotel.

Hotel Orsay - rue, 91-93 Lille. A perfect little hotel (34 rooms. We were in room 31. Nice floral wall paper. A pretty drop leaf table - dark wood. Two chairs - one very French. Both covered in ochre leather. Small. The bath had a sliding door. The bed recessed between two built-in closets.

The staff was so French. Two young men. One young, very short red-haired woman. One older black haired woman. Their cheekbones high - Their beautiful French accented Engl

Notre-Dame

Notre Dame. We got there late Sunday afternoon Mass was just ending — but we were there in time for a splendid organ FINALE. A much lighter, more open church than Chartres.

I prayed again. Both times in thanks for this trip — and for Mark to find his way + for his spirit to be healed. From Harris & Leslie for their marriage to be good — their love to be strong — Harris' health — Leslie's health — For Tom For Kristine that they know joy, satisfaction, peace.

I pray for Mother — for Daddy & Lokie & Carl. I pray for the family of man. All of us. Everywhere. Speaking French, or English, or Spanish or Swahili. That we know & share love.

56

POSTCARDS
19H
18-12
1m
FRANCE

PLACE POSTCARD HERE

PLACE POSTCARD HERE

PLACE POSTCARD HERE

PLACE POSTCARD HERE

PLACE POSTCARD HERE

PLACE POSTCARD HERE

64

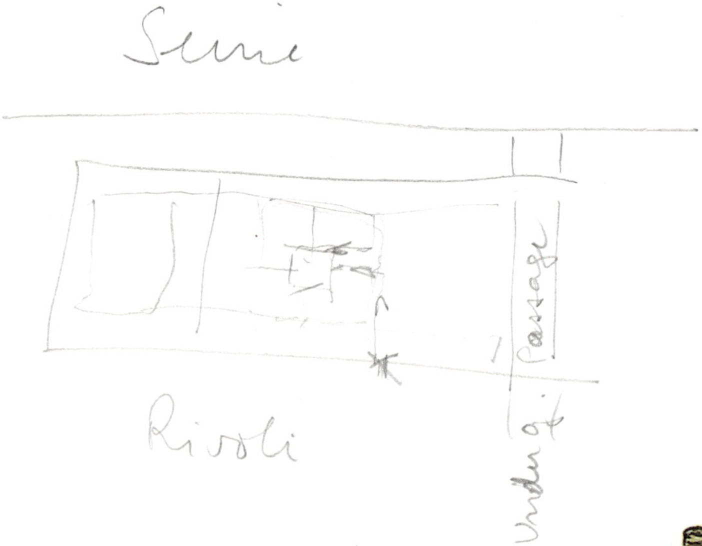
Seine
Passage
Rivoli
Under it

Vianney's drawing of how to go into the side entrance of the Louvre.

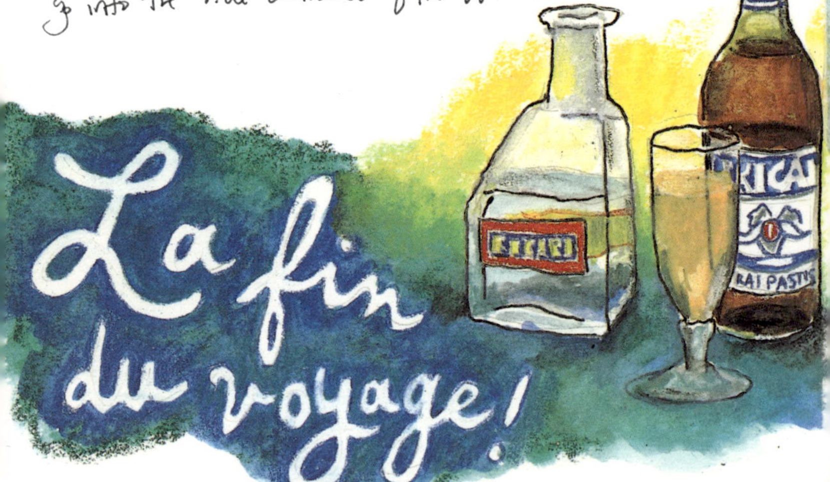
La fin du voyage!
RICA
RAI PASTIS